COSTUME AND FASHION SOURCE BOOKS

The 1950s and 1960s

Anne Rooney

Copyright © 2009 Bailey Publishing Associates Ltd

Produced for Chelsea House by Bailey Publishing Associates Ltd, 11a Woodlands, Hove BN3 6TJ, England

Project Manager: Patience Coster
Text Designer: Jane Hawkins
Picture Research: Shelley Noronha
Artist: Deirdre Clancy Steer

Library of Congress Cataloging-in-Publication Data

Rooney, Anne.
  The 1950s and 1960s / Anne Rooney.
      p. cm. — (Costume source books)
  Includes bibliographical references and index.
  ISBN 978-1-60413-385-1
  1. Fashion—United States—History—20th century—Juvenile literature. 2. Clothing and dress—United States—History—20th century—Juvenile literature. 3. United States—Social life and customs—20th century—Juvenile literature. I. Title. II. Title: Nineteen fifties and sixties. III. Series.

  GT615.R66 2009
  391.009'045—dc22   2008047260

Printed and bound in Hong Kong

10 9 8 7 6 5 4 3 2 1

The publishers would like to thank the following for permission to reproduce their pictures: Bailey Publishing Associates Ltd: *contents page*; Corbis: 5 (© Condé Nast Archive), 6 (© Condé Nast Archive), 7 (© Bettmann), 8 (© Cat's Collection), 9 (© Henry Diltz), 13 (© Bettmann), *title page* and 14 (© Condé Nast Archive), 18 (© Condé Nast Archive), 10 *detail* and 19 (© Condé Nast Archive), 20 (© Condé Nast Archive), 23 (© Bettmann), 26 (© Jack Moebes), 30 (© Michael Ochs Archives), 32 (© Condé Nast Archive), 33 (© Douglas Kirkland), 35 (© Bettmann), 41 (© Henry Diltz), 42 (© Playboy Archive), 43 (© Condé Nast Archive), 44 (© Corbis), 45 (© Bettmann), 46 (© Güttert/dpa), 47 (© Aladdin Color, Inc./Aladdin Color, Inc.), 52 (© Image Source), 53 (© Bettmann), 54 (© Bettmann), 55 (© Henry Diltz), 5 *detail*, 38 *detail* and 56 (© Kate Mitchell/zefa), 59 (© Alan Pappe); Christine Daveau: 22 *detail*; Mary Evans Picture Library: 50; Lisa Gilbert: *imprint and contents pages detail* and 32 *detail*; Kobal Collection: 15, 16, 22, 34 (Paramount), 38 (Danjaq/Eon/UA), 39, 46 *detail* and 48 (Universal), 51 (20th Century Fox), 58 (New Line/The Kobal Collection/ James, David); Mirrorpix: 28; Rex Features: 12, 40; TopFoto: 11 (Land of Lost Content/HIP), 21 (KPA/HIP), 25 (Le Poer Trench Michael/ArenaPAL), 27 (Topham/UPP), 29 (Land of Lost Content/HIP), 36 (Land of Lost Content/HIP); Topham Picturepoint: 10, 24.

Contents

Introduction

In the 1950s and 1960s, fashion magazines were widely available, movies had a mainstream following, and an increasing number of homes were acquiring television sets. More people than ever before could see how the rich and famous dressed. At the same time, cheap, mass-produced clothes began to fill the stores. For the first time, ordinary people could follow fashion and easily align themselves with specific social groups and movements through their choice of clothes.

The 1950s were not very long ago. It's easy to find photos and movies from the period showing clothes exactly as people wore them. Many older people still remember the time and may even have clothes from the era. Be sure to get right what people wore in any theatrical production or re-enactment.

There will be plenty of people around who will say, "It wasn't like that," if you get it wrong!

Between 1950 and 1970, there were many different looks, and fashion changed very quickly and dramatically. This book brings together some of the most popular styles and dominant trends and demonstrates how to achieve the look. Some period pieces can still be found in thrift shops and yard sales. Others can be tracked down via the Internet, where there are auction sites that often have vintage pieces selling for low prices. Other items you can make quite simply. During the 1970s, 1980s, and 1990s, there were revivals of 1950s and 1960s fashions, so if you can't find an original, you can probably find a close copy from a more recent date.

FASHION VICTIM

" *They seek him here, they seek him there,*
His clothes are loud, but never square.
It will make or break him so he's got to buy the best,
'Cause he's a dedicated follower of fashion . . .
Oh yes he is (oh yes he is), oh yes he is (oh yes he is).
There's one thing that he loves and that is flattery.
One week he's in polka-dots, the next week he's
*   in stripes.*
'Cause he's a dedicated follower of fashion. "

Ray Davies, *Dedicated Follower of Fashion* (1966)

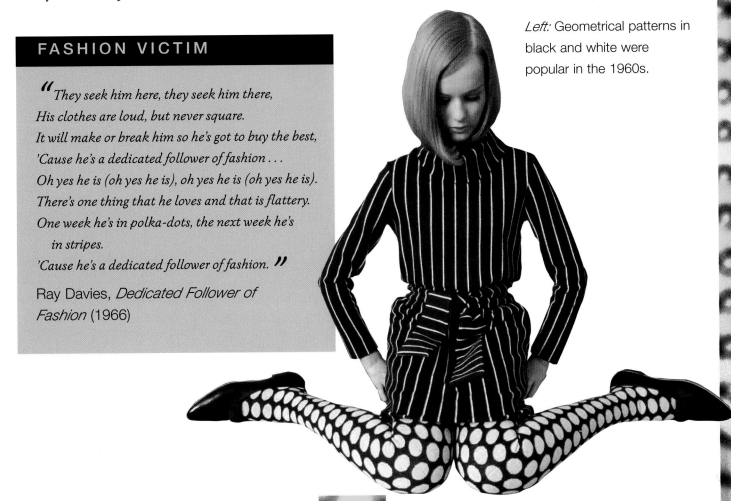

Left: Geometrical patterns in black and white were popular in the 1960s.

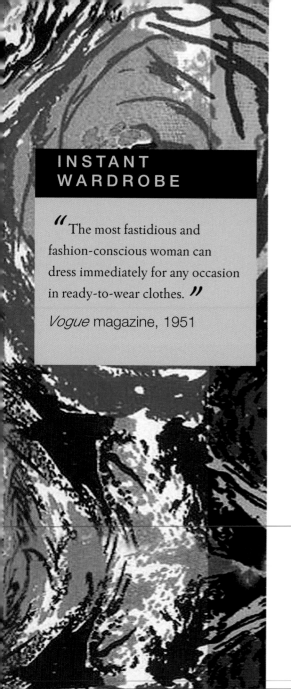

CHAPTER 1

A New Era

EMERGING FROM THE WAR YEARS

During World War II, day-to-day survival was a struggle, and clothing was one of many things in short supply. Fabric and clothing were rationed, and people had to mend and reuse old clothes. Even after the war, clothes rationing continued. But in the 1950s, the fashion scene burst into life, fizzing with color, sensational shapes, and new fibers. It sparked two of the most exciting and fast-moving decades in fashion history, reflecting rapid social change.

Below: In 1953, the American fashion model Suzy Parker was photographed wearing a full skirt and quilted satin jacket. These revolutionary new styles of the post-war years made extravagant use of fabric.

INSTANT WARDROBE

" The most fastidious and fashion-conscious woman can dress immediately for any occasion in ready-to-wear clothes. "

Vogue magazine, 1951

A NEW LOOK FOR A NEW AGE

In 1947, Paris fashion designer Christian Dior launched his revolutionary "New Look" to both searing criticism and rapturous enthusiasm. It was a feminine, sophisticated style with accentuated waists and full skirts. Critics complained that it was unacceptably extravagant to use yards of fabric on a fashion item while some families were so deprived that they could barely feed their children. But after the austerity of the war years, most people wanted to enjoy themselves. Wearing colorful and flamboyant clothes was one way they could express the postwar spirit of exuberance. It was an enthusiasm that was to last throughout the 1950s and 1960s, producing some of the most exciting and original fashions of the twentieth century.

Above: Women go shopping in a New York department store in 1951. For many people, it was still important to find a bargain and keep clothes as long as possible.

REBUILDING THE WEST

The 1950s were a boom time in which many people hoped to live the "American Dream." In the United States, a huge growth in industry caused large, modern factories to spring up across the land. Some of these factories produced clothes and new fabrics. Within a few years of the end of the war, clothes were being mass-produced, and they filled the new department stores. For the first time in history, people other than the very wealthy could afford to own a range of items, not just the few clothes they needed for everyday wear. "Ready-to-wear" collections were launched; a cross between made-to-measure and mass market clothes, they offered a degree of high fashion and exclusivity to people of moderate means.

FABRIC REVOLUTION

Clothes made from new artificial fabrics such as nylon, Courtelle, polyester, and acrylic became popular in the 1950s and 1960s. Easy to care for, they could be washed in the newly popular electric washing machines and could withstand harsh treatment in spin dryers. Many of them did not even need ironing. Women who couldn't afford to buy a lot of clothes could make their own (they'd had plenty of practice during the

CLOTH FROM OIL

Unlike wool, cotton, silk, and linen, artificial fibers are not made from plant or animal material. Instead, they are made in factories from chemicals derived from oil. The first such fabric was nylon, invented in 1935 and used for stockings from 1940. The first polyester fiber, Terylene, was invented in 1941. When polyester clothes were first sold in the United States, in 1951, the advertisements called polyester a "miracle" fiber that could be worn for 68 days without ironing and still look presentable!

war years). Sewing machines and knitting machines quickly became popular. All a woman needed to keep up with the latest trends was some fabric, a paper pattern, and a sewing machine.

INTO THE SPACE AGE

The spirit of optimism grew throughout the 1950s and into the 1960s. The launch of the first satellite in 1957 and the first man in space in 1961 sparked public enthusiasm for technology and started the "space race." The USSR had been the first country to send a man into space, but the U.S. was determined to be first to put a man on the moon. In the 1960s, the obsession with all things space-related touched many aspects of daily life, including fashion. The fabrics used for clothing became more outlandish and experimental—plastics, paper, and metal featured in clothes that were often impractical and sometimes barely wearable. Science-fiction movies and television shows such as *Star Trek, Lost in Space, 2001: A Space Odyssey*, and *Barbarella* showed tight jumpsuits and shiny, metallic fabrics that were soon copied in real life.

LIBERATION

The 1960s were marked, too, by social revolution. The invention of the contraceptive pill put women in charge of their sexual life for the first time by allowing them to control their fertility. Taking strides into public life and toward social equality, they chose clothes that suited a more liberated lifestyle. Many women rebelled against conventional attitudes by ditching skirts and wearing pants that gave them greater freedom of movement. The Civil Rights Act of 1964 meant that black people began to move toward equality with white people in the United States. The styles and attitudes of black activists, actors, and musicians began to have an impact on white culture, including fashion.

Both women and men began to challenge the rigid gender roles that held sway in the 1950s. It gradually became more acceptable to be homosexual, get divorced, and enjoy sex outside of marriage. Late in the 1960s, men adopted more

Left: This fantasy costume from the film *Barbarella* (1968) shows actor Jane Fonda in popular space-age styling.

flamboyant fabrics, colors, and styles that would have been considered dangerously effeminate in the previous decade. They wore figure-hugging clothes, flounces, frills, bright colors, and patterns not seen in men's costume since the eighteenth century.

ANOTHER REVOLUTION

In the later 1960s, the spirit of optimism gave way to disenchantment. A long-running war in Vietnam, together with the Cold War and the nuclear arms race, contributed to disillusionment with the modern world. Fashion became nostalgic, taking its cue from the early twentieth century and featuring long, flowing skirts, frills, and flounces. Hippies found inspiration in Eastern philosophies, particularly from India, and swapped garish fluorescents and metallics for ethnic clothes made from natural fabrics and colored with vegetable dyes. Artificial fibers gave way to cotton, linen, hemp, and wool as young people became cynical of big business, technology, and the status quo.

STYLE TIP

In the 1960s, a person's political beliefs could often be read from his or her clothes. This makes the clothing chosen for a play or re-enactment particularly important. The students who rioted in Paris often wore the "beatnik" style of black, while American protesters against the Vietnam War might wear flamboyant and flowery hippie or "romantic" clothing. So remember to match your costume appropriately if you are staging one of these events.

Left: In the 1960s, people who rejected mainstream values often showed their different stance in their choice of "rebellious" clothing.

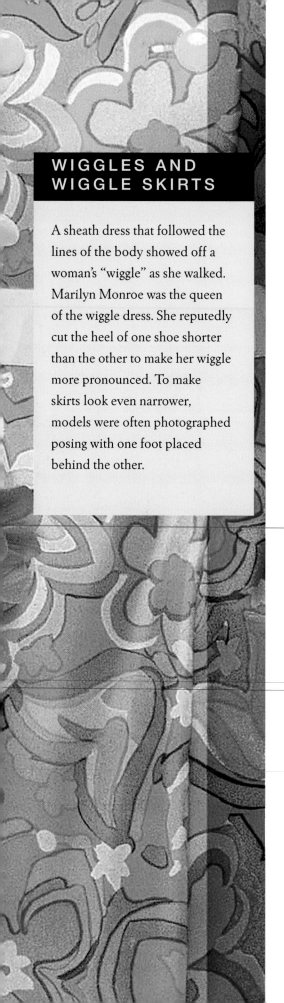

CHAPTER 2

Women's Day Wear

WIGGLES AND WIGGLE SKIRTS

A sheath dress that followed the lines of the body showed off a woman's "wiggle" as she walked. Marilyn Monroe was the queen of the wiggle dress. She reputedly cut the heel of one shoe shorter than the other to make her wiggle more pronounced. To make skirts look even narrower, models were often photographed posing with one foot placed behind the other.

A SCULPTURAL STYLE

During the 1950s and 1960s, women's fashions were transformed from sharp, geometric shapes in artificial fabrics to free-flowing lines in natural fibers. And although most people did not slavishly follow fashion, the new designs filtered down, in a diluted form, to the ordinary woman on the street. In the early 1950s, fashion gave a woman's body a sculptural look with extreme geometric lines, contrasting colors, and striking asymmetry. It was realized in one of two ways—either with wide, triangular jackets, tent coats, and dresses or in a constricted shape, which squeezed the body into the narrowest silhouette possible.

STAYING WITH THE NEW LOOK

The New Look had rounded shoulders and a fitted top pulled in to accentuate the waist; it then flared out into a long, wide skirt. In everyday wear, this shape was easily achieved with either a dress or a skirt and

Above: The style of formal day wear in the 1950s was carefully researched for the Todd Haynes movie *Far from Heaven* (2002).

shirt. Summer dresses were often made of printed cotton, polyester, or chiffon and topped with a fine-knit, waist-length cardigan. The bodice was closely fitted, either with a shirt-style buttoned front or a wide slash neck. The skirt was gathered or pleated onto the waistband. In winter, a costume of a skirt and jacket made of tweed or Courtelle, maybe in a plain color or plaid, was coupled with a tailored shirt.

If an appropriate dress or suit is not available, a wide skirt in a plain or floral fabric may be teamed with a fitted blouse, either with a flat collar or buttoned to the neck and finished with a bow. Careful use of accessories such as beads, hat, gloves, shoes, and handbag can make the look convincing. For the ambitious, there are many surviving dress and suit patterns from the 1950s, but they are often quite challenging to make. A shirt can be given a 1950s shape by adding darts to make it fitted—although many of today's shirts are already a suitable, tailored shape.

LONG AND LEAN

An alternative style, which required less fabric, was the I-line. Here, a fitted bodice was paired with a pencil-slim skirt. The outfit hugged the body from the shoulders to several inches below the knee. The most fashionable I-line costumes were sophisticated sheath dresses. The addition of a wide-brimmed hat, long gloves, a cigarette holder, and

Right: A slim-line linen suit was an elegant choice for a woman in the 1950s, especially when finished with gloves and hat.

CRIMPLENE

Invented in the early 1950s, Crimplene quickly became popular as a "wonder" fabric. It was a heavy, easy-care fabric that held its shape well and did not wrinkle. It was named after the Crimple Valley near Harrogate in northern England, where the manufacturer ICI had its factory. Crimplene was hugely popular during the 1950s and 1960s but fell out of favor in the 1970s when people returned to natural fibers.

NEW COLORS

The new, washable, and drip-dry fabrics meant that for the first time, ordinary people could wear clean clothes every day. To exploit this advantage and mark a break with the deeper and often drabber shades of the past, many 1950s clothes were in pale colors. Sweaters in artificial yarns such as acrylic could be machine-washed, so people were able to wear white or pastels to work and on public transportation without having to worry about getting their clothes dirty.

the new stiletto-heeled shoes made the style all the more elegant. A matching short jacket worn over the dress would have three-quarter-length sleeves.

A modern shift dress may not have the right neckline, which should ideally be a slash or a shallow scoop. If you can't adjust the neckline, hide it with a knotted scarf. The skirt should be just on, or below the knees—

you may be able to let down the hem but if not, sew a band of contrasting fabric to the hem. You could add a contrasting band to the neckline as well. Stretchy fabrics were not widely used for dresses in the 1950s—instead, the slender profile was achieved with tailoring. But a modern stretchy dress would make a reasonable substitute to re-create the look.

HIDING THE BODY

A contrasting trend was for voluminous jackets, coats, and dresses, which fell in folds from the shoulders or a yoke. Sometimes a roomy, triangular, or balloon-shaped jacket was teamed with a knife-sharp pencil skirt or tapered pants, but at other times the entire outfit was shapeless and huge.

This is an easy look to re-create with a mid-calf pencil skirt or skinny, tailored, or stretch pants topped with a wide swing coat or roomy top. Maternity clothes can provide an easy way of achieving the "tent dress" look.

SWEATER GIRLS

Until the 1950s, people between the ages of 15 and 20 had simply been regarded as young adults. But the 1950s saw the coining of a new term—teenager. For the first time, young people wanted, and got, their own fashions. New trends started in the street and worked their way into the pages of fashion magazines.

Many girls wore slim, tapered pants, often with a high waist, and paired these with a figure-hugging sweater. Some styles of pants stopped above the ankles; capri pants were cut off at mid-calf. Pants were frequently made in artificial fibers.

Sweaters could be close-fitting and short, extending just to the waist. They were sometimes worn with a matching cardigan in a "twinset." Or they were oversized in chunky knits, often with dropped armholes, which created bat-wing sleeves. This "sloppy Joe" sweater hid the shape of the upper body, while the legs were defined in narrow, tapered pants. The sweater may have had a roll neck, but if it had a V-neck, this was often filled in with a scarf, rows of pearls, or beads. Flat shoes and hair tied back in a ponytail completed the casual look. Today, tapered pants cut off above the ankle can be teamed with a large man's sweater.

Right: Marilyn Monroe shows off her curves in a popular informal combination of sweater and tight pants.

Above: An A-line dress hides the woman's figure, but its simplicity is offset by the large hat and jewelry.

THE A-LINE DRESS

The A-line took the United States by storm when it was adopted by President John F. Kennedy's wife, Jackie, in the early 1960s. From narrow shoulders, it marked the waist only slightly—if at all—and widened considerably over the hips and thighs, making the shape of the letter *A*. Jackie Kennedy paired a neat, A-line dress with a pillbox hat, gloves, heels, and makeup. To be perfect, everything had to match—dress, jacket, shoes, hat, and gloves. Fabrics had to be stiff enough to keep the shape of the *A* rather than just drape over the body. Linen was popular, as were some of the stiffer artificial fabrics, including Crimplene. Sometimes a matching A-line coat was worn over the dress, with a small collar or no collar at all and close-fitting sleeves. A more extreme shape, the trapeze dress, was even more triangular. It did not mark the waist at all, but flared outward from the shoulders.

The A-line dress has a simple shape and is quite easy to make if you can't find a ready-made version. Choose a thick fabric that will hold its shape. Furnishing fabrics are useful. Detailing should be kept simple, with buttons in the same color or fabric. A bow in the same fabric stitched under the bust was a common feature.

FALLING WAISTLINES AND RISING HEMLINES

During the early 1960s, dresses grew slowly shorter and more rectangular. Some had a dropped waist and a skirt gathered or pleated onto the hips; others were shifts or tunics with little shape at all. Suits, too, were quite rectangular, with a straight skirt and a boxy jacket with three-quarter-length sleeves and either no collar or a flat, Peter Pan collar.

THE MINI

When Paris fashion designer Yves St. Laurent first showed catwalk models wearing skirts above the knee in the late 1950s, there was an outcry from the shocked public. But the die had been cast, and skirts continued to rise. By the mid-1960s, the miniskirt had become the style of the moment. As a dress, it was often a simple, rectangular tunic or pinafore dress, worn over a shirt or close-fitting sweater by day or on its own in the evening. As a skirt, it was again simple and straight and was matched with a shirt or sweater. The miniskirt sat on the hips rather than fitting round the waist and was often worn with a wide belt in shiny white or colored plastic.

Right: Raquel Welch poses in a minidress. Its simple styling and plain color are typical of the time.

PAPER CLOTHING

In 1967, disposable paper clothing was briefly in vogue. Because paper clothing was made with few seams, the shapes were inevitably simple, such as the A-line or tunic dress, and the clothes were not fitted to the body. The paper could be cheaply printed in bright colors and patterns. Paper clothing can be made from strong, fabric-based wrapping paper, which is flexible and does not tear easily. The stiffness of paper clothing and the noise it made when the wearer moved around meant it was popular only briefly.

Right: Marisa Tomei wears a simple coat in a bold color in the movie *Alfie* (2004). A coat like this would often be made from an artificial fabric, such as Crimplene.

POP ART AND OP ART

The pop art movement began in the 1950s and flourished in the 1960s. It used images from popular culture and everyday life. Some of the most famous examples of pop art are Andy Warhol's pictures of Campbell's soup cans and Roy Lichtenstein's oversized strip cartoon images. Op art features geometric patterns that often produce optical illusions—such as the black-and-white images of British artist Bridget Riley. Both pop art and op art patterns were used on fabrics and for clothing in the 1960s. Some dresses featured a single large design—a stylized part of a face or one flower, for example. Others used op art patterns to produce a dizzying effect in tune with the rising use of hallucinogenic drugs.

Coats were a similar boxy shape, often with a Peter Pan collar and prominent buttons. Many had three-quarter-length sleeves. The popular "scooter" coat was straight or A-line, and was often made of brightly colored PVC.

A mini-tunic or pinafore is easy to make or can be achieved by shortening the skirt of a pinafore dress. To adapt a jacket or coat, choose one with a straight shape and shorten the sleeves. Remove the collar and cut a rounded neck. Add large, flat, round buttons. A child's plastic raincoat in a bright color can be adapted to make a scooter coat, if you can find one large enough—it doesn't matter if the coat or the sleeves are too short.

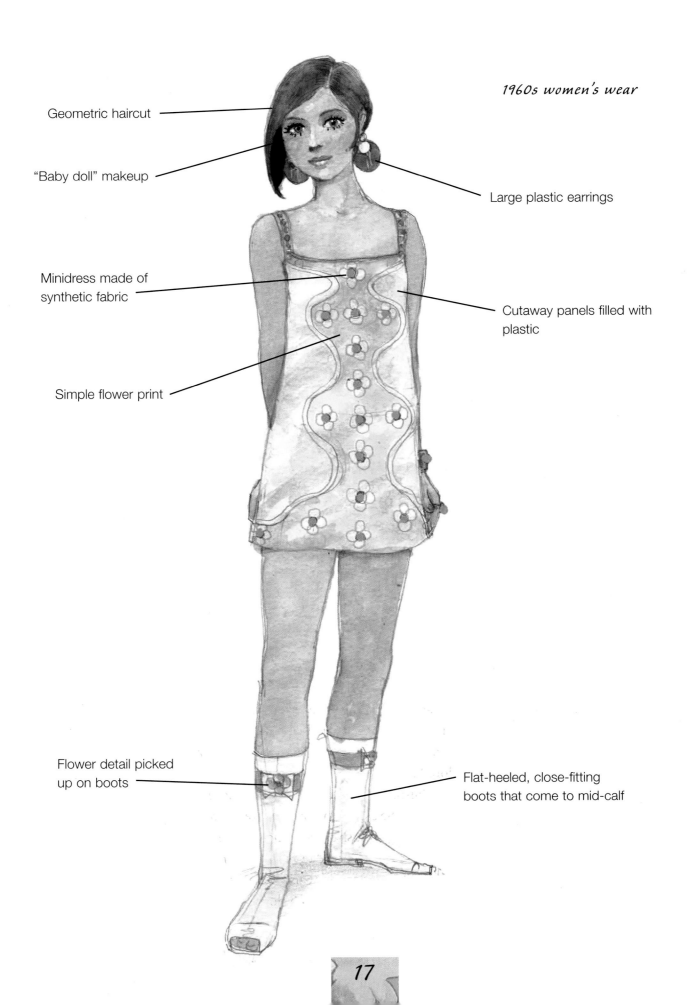

Geometric haircut

"Baby doll" makeup

1960s women's wear

Large plastic earrings

Minidress made of
synthetic fabric

Cutaway panels filled with
plastic

Simple flower print

Flower detail picked
up on boots

Flat-heeled, close-fitting
boots that come to mid-calf

17

SHORTER AND SHORTER

From the mid-1960s, hemlines rose higher and higher until the miniskirt stopped at the top of the thighs, briefly becoming the microskirt. Then the microskirt split into shorts, which, by 1970, were known as hot pants. These could be in functional wool flannel or tweed—or in futuristic fabrics such as PVC.

COLOR AND PATTERN

While shapes were simple, color and pattern added interest to clothes. Vivid colors were popular, moving from pastels in the early 1960s to bright poster colors and then more vibrant and daring fluorescents in

Right: Career girls in New York City in the 1960s, wearing minidresses and with bobbed hair.

acid green, yellow, orange, and pink. Colors often clashed—orange was worn with purple or lime green with maroon. Patterns were starkly geometric, with large blocks of primary colors, or borrowed from op art, with zigzags, stripes, and optical illusions in black and white.

PSYCHEDELIA

In the second half of the 1960s, geometric designs gave way to kaleidoscopic patterns in gaudy fluorescent or acid colors. The new chaotic and asymmetrical patterns of psychedelic colors formed a style known as "pyschedelia." The designs drew inspiration from the highly glamorized drug culture. The mind-altering drugs marijuana and LSD grew in popularity during the 1960s and were commonly depicted in popular culture. The colors and patterns of psychedelia were intended to simulate the use of psychotropic drugs. Bold, imaginative, swirling patterns merged into one another. Fluorescent purple was very much associated with this style, and it was used with other bright primary and secondary colors to dazzling effect. Fabrics were often luminous, sometimes with a shiny surface, such as satin; they also tended to be soft and fluid, marking a move away from the hard surfaces and sharp lines of the space-age look.

CATSUITS

The opposite of loose, boxy clothes—skintight catsuits—copied the futuristic outfits shown in science-fiction movies and TV shows. Only the most perfect body looked good in these stretchy, brightly colored suits, the waist accented with a wide belt. The catsuit look can be copied with stretchy dance wear, accessorized with a belt and boots.

Right: A model wears a plastic raincoat in bright colors with a psychedelic "flower power" pattern. Note the opaque, knee-high socks.

Right: In 1967, a *Vogue* model is photographed wearing a floaty "baby doll" dress in yellow Indian cotton.

BABY DOLL LOOK

A vogue for "baby doll" dresses played on the very youthful look that was fashionable. Girls wore short dresses, often with puffed sleeves and the skirt gathered into a high "empire" waistline just under the bust. Colors were pastel, patterns floral, and girls wore their hair long and loose.

THE HIPPIE LOOK

The "summer of love" in 1967 was the height of the hippie movement in fashion, music, and lifestyle. Men and women wore their hair long and their clothes loose, ethnic, deliberately unstyled and anti-fashion. In a rebellion against the consumerism of the 1950s and 1960s, young people shunned anything produced or promoted by big business corporations and adopted a "natural" look. They opposed nuclear weapons, the war in Vietnam, and middle-class values and preached a doctrine of peace and love. Their clothes were made from natural fabrics, by traditional methods, and borrowed from ethnic styles around the world, including loose kaftans, Indian printed silks and cottons, and techniques such as tie-dye and batik. Fibers included cotton, hemp, wool (sometimes homespun), cheesecloth, and sheepskin.

Women wore wraparound skirts in coarse cotton, often block-printed with vegetable dyes in deep red, brown, ocher, and green. Skirts often reached the ankles. Above the skirt, a loose smock or shirt, frequently made of cheesecloth, was common. There might be a chunky sweater or long cardigan if it was cold, but shawls were widely used as well. Sweaters and shawls were often homemade, using traditional crafts such as knitting, crochet, and macramé. The look is easily re-created, since ethnic clothing of the same styles is still widely available.

ROMANTICS

Not only hippies turned to longer skirts. In the mainstream, too, disillusionment with the present led to a nostalgic look that borrowed from the early years of the century, with long "maxi" skirts, frilled blouses with high necks, and long velvet coats. These were often worn with lace-up ankle boots and floppy hats. Long, loose hair was given a pre-Raphaelite look by braiding it when wet.

PANTYHOSE

The large expanse of leg revealed beneath the miniskirt or hot pants was sheathed in a new invention—pantyhose. Before the 1960s, girls and women had worn stockings held up by garters. But one-piece pantyhose meant that short skirts no longer posed a problem to a girl's modesty. These garments came in different colors and even with printed patterns or woven textures. Often, thick wool pantyhose were worn with boots that could come to anywhere between mid-calf and lower thigh.

MAKE IT—A TIE-DYED TOP

Wash a cotton T-shirt and tie the wet shirt in knots, or twist it and secure the folds with rubber bands. Mix a pack of dye according to the instructions. Soak the shirt in the dye for at least 20 minutes, then rinse it in cold water until the water runs clear. Undo the knots, rinse the shirt again, then allow it to dry.

Left: Actor Kate Winslet wears the hippie look in the film *Hideous Kinky* (1998), set in Morocco in the 1960s.

Men's Day Wear

CIVILIAN CLOTHING

At the end of World War II, men looked drab. Those who were demobilized (had left the armed forces) were issued a set of "civvies"—basic civilian clothing, which included a suit, shirt, shoes, socks, tie, raincoat, and hat. Men not in the armed forces often chose to give their clothing coupons to their wives rather than buy new clothes themselves.

Over the next 25 years, men's costume would be transformed. During the 1950s, the popularity of casual wear such as jeans, slacks, and shorts increased along with the sharp formality of dudes on the one hand and neo-Edwardians on the other. Another transformation occurred during the 1960s, resulting in clothing that the demobilized men of 1945 would have considered unacceptably informal and effeminate.

Below: Teenage boys in the 1950s, as epitomized by the Nelson brothers, wear casual slacks and knitwear.

DAILY ROUTINE

Most ordinary men in the 1950s wore unremarkable clothes. In the United States, conscription meant that many young men spent a lot of time in uniform. Out of uniform, they wore slacks and single-breasted blazers, usually with a plain white shirt and a narrow tie. The look was neat and groomed, almost a uniform in itself. Trousers had lots of fabric in the leg; they also had cuffs and were held up with suspenders. Many men wore a tie, even when not at work.

A casual look popularized by movie stars such as Rock Hudson, Steve McQueen, and Dean Martin combined loose, wool flannel pants, a patterned short-sleeved shirt or polo shirt, and loafers—low-heeled, slip-on shoes. The shirt could be checked, striped, or more flamboyantly patterned. A cardigan, sweater, or sweater vest might be worn, too.

THE RISE OF THE TEENAGER

The 1950s belonged to the newly emerging teenagers. Although the fashions of teenage rebels were worn by relatively few people at the time, they loom large in the collective memory of the 1950s. The intoxicating influence of music and movie stars such as Elvis Presley, James Dean, and Marlon Brando offered young men icons from whom they could copy an alternative look to that of the clean-cut "boy next door."

In the early 1950s, stylish men around Mayfair in London adopted clothing reminiscent of Edwardian finery. Their single-breasted coats had velvet collars and were worn with narrow black trousers, horizontally striped shirts with stiff white collars, and bowler hats. Suit jackets had four buttons and were worn over a vest with small lapels. It was a tailored, expensive, and nostalgic look.

TEDDY BOYS

This neo-Edwardian look was soon transformed by the teddy boys, a youth culture that grew out of the streets of South London. Teddy boys turned the knee-length, single-breasted coat into the "drape," a fitted coat made of wool with velvet or satin detailing at the lapels and cuffs, and lots

---

Right: Photographed performing on stage in the mid-1960s, actor and "crooner" Dean Martin wears casual clothes, including a flat-collared shirt and cardigan.

FAIR ISLE

Knitted vests were frequently made following a traditional pattern called Fair Isle, which uses horizontal bands of small geometric shapes in different colors. It required only small quantities of wool in any single color. Fair Isle sweaters were often made using wool unraveled from old garments, including socks, and were a good way to recycle yarn at a time when people had little money.

SHOE FETISH

" *You can burn my house,*
Steal my car,
Drink my liquor
From an old fruit jar.
Do anything that you want to do,
*   but uh-uh,*
Honey, lay off of my shoes
Don't you step on my blue suede
*   shoes.*
Well you can do anything but lay
*   off of my blue suede shoes.* "

Carl Perkins, *Blue Suede Shoes* (sung by Elvis Presley, 1956)

of pockets. They paired it with narrow pants in the same or a different color and often with a brocade vest and stiff shirt. The shirt might be white or a dark, plain color and was worn with a narrow or shoelace "slim Jim" tie. Their shoes were suede with thick crepe soles. Their hair was long with a pompadour, held in place by Brylcreem and worn with long sideburns. The look was a strange blend of aggression, narcissism, and style.

Today, the drape can be created from a narrow knee-length coat by stitching velvet onto the lapels and cuffs. If there are not enough pockets, add velvet pocket flaps to simulate extra ones. Trousers should be a matching color—pale drainpipes can be dyed with fabric dye.

GREASERS

The greaser look initially grew out of styles worn by working-class youths in the eastern states of the United States. They wore white or black T-shirts with the sleeves rolled up, or a white tank top, often with a dark-colored work jacket or trench coat. Also popular were Sir Guy or Daddy-O shirts—these were short-sleeved shirts with a turned-back, flat collar, often in black with vertical panels of a contrasting color on either side of the front opening. A modern bowling shirt is a good substitute. Leather motorcycle jackets with the collar turned up or Levi's denim jackets were popular alternatives to the work jacket.

Greasers wore jeans, preferably Levi's 501 or 505, with the cuff turned back four inches (10 centimeters), or baggy cotton twill work pants, usually in sand, dark blue, or gray. Twill pants soon appeared in a wide range of colors, including orange and lime green. Footwear ranged from pointed Italian shoes through creepers and Converse All Star sneakers to motorcycle boots and army boots. A narrow-brimmed hat or flat cap was also popular.

Below: Leather jackets, white T-shirts, and tight jeans—a 1950s uniform worn on stage in the musical *Grease*.

BLUE JEANS

Jeans first became popular in the 1850s among mine workers in California. A century later, they became the uniform for a generation of young people. At first they were seen as nonconformist and aggressive—some social venues banned people wearing jeans—but that only added to their appeal. Jeans were favored by greasers but by the late 1950s and early 1960s were being worn by many people.

The greaser look is easy to achieve. The jeans must be narrow, with the bottom of the leg rolled up, and they should be worn with boots, a white T-shirt (perhaps under a shirt left open at the neck), and a black leather biker jacket.

BEATNIKS AND BUMS

The anarchic beat culture that emerged in the late 1950s was rebellious and radical, inspired by jazz music and rejecting American materialism and capitalist politics. Beatniks had a distinctive look characterized by close-fitting black turtleneck sweaters or T-shirts, worn with jeans. They also wore oversized chunky knit sweaters in plain, dark colors.

Distinctive details were a small goatee beard, open-toed leather sandals, a beret, and sunglasses. Men and women in the beat movement often dressed entirely in black. Women's beatnik fashions included black leotards and wearing their hair long, straight and unadorned in a rebellion against the middle-class culture of beauty salons.

ENDLESS BLACK

"The beat look is the news at Dior . . . pale zombie faces; leather suits and coats; knitted caps and high turtleneck collars, black endlessly."
Vogue magazine, 1960

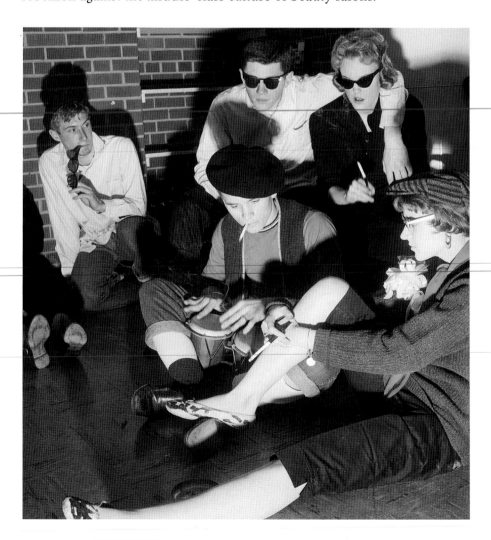

Right: For 1950s beatniks, berets and dark glasses were vital accessories. At the time, smoking was seen as a "cool" activity. Re-enactors today can use dummy cigarettes to capture the look.

Above: The Beatles—Paul McCartney, John Lennon, Ringo Starr and George Harrison (left to right)—seen here wearing their trademark collarless suits by designer Pierre Cardin.

THE LONDON LOOK

In the 1960s, London became the center of the fashion world. The term "Swinging London" was coined to describe the dynamic changes of the time and the city that appeared to be at the heart of this revolution. The fashion designer, Mary Quant, and the model Twiggy, with her tiny frame, mod-cropped hair and miniskirts, came to symbolize the youth movement that was associated with Swinging London. The British Union Jack flag became a fashion feature on coats, dresses, hats and bags.

The Beatles, a Liverpudlian pop group who rose to fame in 1962–63, were closely associated with the London look. The four band members wore impeccable dark suits with boxy jackets and narrow lapels. Under the jacket, they wore a white shirt with a small collar and narrow tie. Later, they wore suits designed for them by Pierre Cardin, which had distinctive collarless jackets with rounded necks. Their pants were narrow drainpipes, often worn over short boots. The Beatle look was an adaptation of the mod look, and it was widely copied all around the world. Men soon wore dark, close-fitting sweaters with their drainpipes. They were dapper and stylish, with a clean, slim outline.

STYLE TIP

No 1960s re-enactment would be complete without hot pants. These "short shorts" are very tight and spectacularly brief, with a maximum inseam length of 2 inches (about 6 centimeters). Long legs are an asset to hot pants wearers, as are dark, heavy-denier pantyhose!

UNISEX CLOTHES

Some looks, such as flared pants and frilly shirts, were "unisex," worn by both men and women. Shops selling unisex clothes opened first in the fashionable areas of London around Carnaby Street, Camden Town, and Chelsea.

MODS AND ROCKERS

In Britain in the early 1960s, two rival teen cultures, mods and rockers, were in conflict. The rockers were similar to the American greasers. They rode motorcycles, wore leather jackets, and cultivated a hard, masculine image. Items of rocker clothing, such as black leather biker jackets, are still current. The mods rode scooters, wore clean-cut designer suits, and adopted an air of sophistication. Mods protected their suits with a trademark coat, the parka. This was a long, baggy, padded jacket with a fur-trimmed hood, an army surplus item that was cheap and practical.

SKINHEADS

The most hard-line followers of the mod movement took the style a step further: these "skinheads" looked scary and at times displayed aggressive behavior. They wore jeans, Fred Perry sportswear, and a Ben Sherman shirt with a button-down collar. They included details such as inch-wide suspenders, Dr. Martens lace-up boots, sweater vests, and cardigans. True to their name, skinheads cropped their hair very short.

Right: Skinheads adopted an aggressive look with very short haircuts and suspenders.

DR. MARTENS

When the German doctor Klaus Maertens developed a modified army boot with an air-cushioned sole to support an injured ankle, he hit on a style that would become an important fashion accessory. In 1960, he added yellow stitching to the red leather boot, anglicized the name to Dr. Martens, and released his design onto the UK market. It was an instant success. DMs, as they soon became known, later appeared in a range of colors and in a 14-hole style as well as the original eight hole. They were central to the skinhead look.

Skinheads wore their jeans turned back several inches into deep cuffs to show off their boots. The jeans were often bleached, which skinheads achieved by just spilling bleach on them. This is easy to copy, but remember to wash the bleach off when the color fades and before the fabric disintegrates! (Always remember to wear rubber gloves and handle bleach with care; it can cause serious skin burns.) A thick tartan or check shirt over a white T-shirt and Dr. Martens boots will complete the look.

HIPPIES

In the late 1960s, the "peace and love" ethos of the hippie movement emerged as a counterbalance to the aggressive stance of the skinheads. Men's hippie clothing, like that of women, took its inspiration from ethnic garments around the world. Kaftans—long loose robes with wide sleeves—were borrowed from Morocco. Shirts were often wide and loose, with voluminous sleeves and no cuffs or collar. They were decorated with embroidery or beads. T-shirts remained popular, often with batik or tie-dyed patterns or printed with logos, slogans, and artistic designs. Men went barefoot or wore open-toed leather sandals.

Hippies wore their hair long and were comfortable wearing beads and other jewelry, especially if it had an ethnic flavor. Coats and loose vests were long and made of ornate fabrics such as brocade and velvet or were knitted or crocheted from yarn. Particularly popular at the end of the 1960s and into the 1970s was the huge, shaggy Afghan coat. This was made from sheepskin, with the fur on the inside but showing prominently at the hem, cuffs, neck, and front opening. It was often decorated with embroidery around the cuffs, hem, and front opening.

Make flared pants by slitting the leg seam of a pair of pants such as jeans from the ankle to the knee and stitching in a

---

Right: The hippie look allowed men to wear effeminate-looking clothes and have long hair, challenging conventional ideas about gender roles.

MAKE IT—A HIPPIE VEST

Cut three rectangles of fabric, one for the back and two narrower ones for the front panels. They should be long enough to reach from shoulder to mid-thigh. Shape armholes and the front opening, then stitch the front panels to the back at the shoulders and under the arms. The use of felt as a fabric avoids the need to hem the edges.

triangle of contrasting fabric (use paisley print to look authentically "hippie"). Kaftans take little skill to sew since they are unfitted and made of simple, straight shapes.

PEACOCKS

More flamboyant styles and colors began to appear in men's fashions from the middle of the 1960s, leading to the label "peacocks" for the men who wore them. Shirts sprouted ruffles and frills at the front and the cuffs and had voluminous sleeves. They could be in any color, including lime green, orange, yellow, pink, and lilac, and in swirling psychedelic patterns or flamboyant florals. Necks were finished with a cravat. It was a blatantly effeminate style. Jackets with wide lapels returned, and pants grew wider. Drainpipes gave way to flares or loons—pants that were narrow and figure-hugging at the top but flared below the knee. They sat on the hips, often held up with a wide belt.

Below: The Rolling Stones adopted some of the flamboyant styles of the late 1960s. The ornate jacket worn by Mick Jagger (seated on the left) is typical of "peacock" styling.

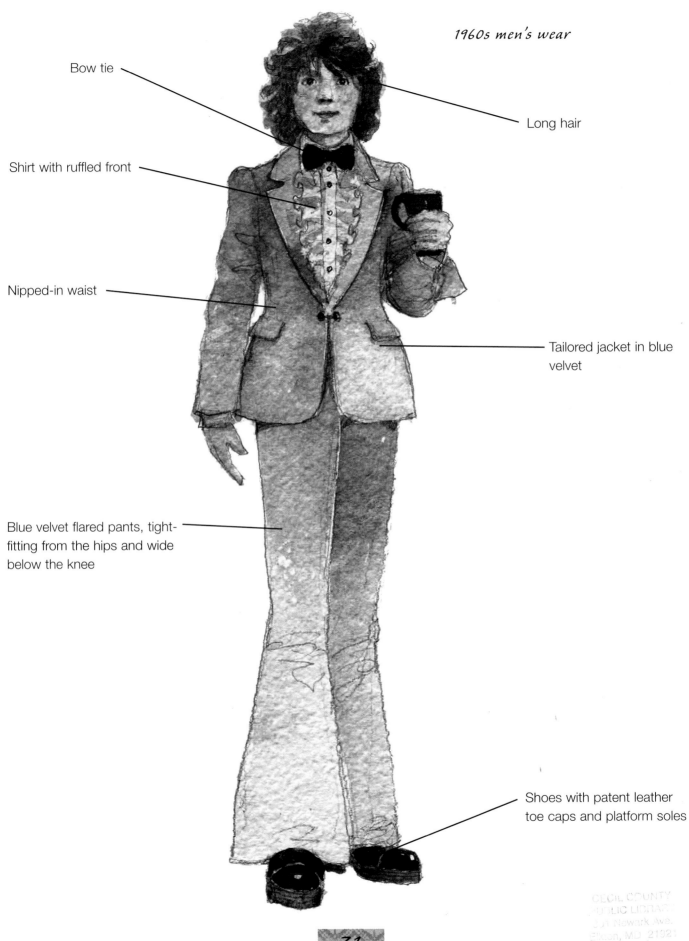

1960s men's wear

Bow tie

Long hair

Shirt with ruffled front

Nipped-in waist

Tailored jacket in blue velvet

Blue velvet flared pants, tight-fitting from the hips and wide below the knee

Shoes with patent leather toe caps and platform soles

CHAPTER 4

Women's Formal and Evening Dress

ITALIAN GLAMOR

" She wore a big, longish, striped skirt and a black tight-fitting jacket and a large, black velvet, broad-brimmed hat tilted far back on her head. "

Iris Murdoch, *The Italian Girl* (1962)

Above: Smart suits continued into the 1960s as elegant day wear, but the shape was straighter and the skirt shorter than in the 1950s.

The shapes of everyday dresses were exaggerated even more for women's formal and evening wear. If the daytime silhouette was slim, the evening silhouette was blade thin. If in the daytime a woman wore a wide skirt, in the evening it may well have ballooned to astonishing proportions. Shape was of primary importance in the 1950s, and fabrics were chosen to make the shapes possible.

DAYTIME FINERY

Although women seldom held important positions in business, wealthier women often wore sharply tailored suits to the races, to charity functions, or just to shop and lunch with other ladies of leisure. Jackets often fit tightly to the waist, were single-breasted, and had small lapels and either full-length or three-quarter-length sleeves. The skirt was narrow and sometimes even tapered in. This made it hard to walk, so the skirt was often slashed at the back or had a kick pleat. Alternatively, a full, closely pleated skirt was worn with a less formally styled jacket—without lapels, and sometimes without buttons. If the suit was made of patterned fabric, it would be plaid or houndstooth or a similar traditional pattern. The look was completed, always, with heels, gloves, and a hat. Hair was tidy, gathered into a chignon or cut short with no stray tendrils to distract from the clean lines.

Formal clothes were expensive, so convertible outfits were popular. Sleeveless sheath dresses often came with a matching jacket, making them respectable and smart for daytime; a woman could remove the jacket to achieve a more dramatic look for the evening.

The combination of a skirt or dress with a jacket remained a popular choice for formal day wear in the 1960s. A-line dresses were often paired with either a matching short collarless jacket or a matching full-length coat, which was the same length as the dress itself. The coat was A-line too and usually had a round neck and no collar. Sometimes a sleeveless coat (like a long vest) in a thicker fabric and coordinating color was worn with a patterned, long-sleeved dress in one of the thinner, artificial fabrics such as rayon or polyester.

PANTSUITS

In the 1960s, pantsuits for women appeared for both day wear and evening wear. Initially, there was much social resistance. Women going out in the evening in pantsuits were often turned away from hotels and restaurants as unsuitably dressed. Formal wear during the 1960s was becoming less formal, but it still took a while for society to catch up with fashion.

While pantsuits for day wear sometimes copied styles and fabrics from men's suits, those for evening wear were often in vibrant colors, in satin or silk. They had a tailored jacket or

Below: The French actor and style icon Brigitte Bardot poses in a characteristically nonchalant, mussed-up style. This 1960s photo shows her wearing a mustard yellow pantsuit and matching cap, with a plain sweater and flat lace-up shoes.

Right: Audrey Hepburn in a 1950s evening dress with a fitted bodice and narrow skirt, worn with a wrap of the same fabric and long gloves.

sleeveless tunic over wide trousers. A satin pantsuit for evening could be made now by adapting satin pajamas, removing the sleeves and buttons, and stitching up the front opening to make a tunic—and perhaps wearing it back to front.

COCKTAIL HOUR

Evening dresses in the 1950s were often cut from a stiff fabric, which would hold the all-important shape. Taffeta or brocade no longer had to be made from silk, since the new artificial fibers were cheaper and easy to clean. The shapes were similar to those of day dresses but even more exaggerated. A close-fitting sheath dress would have a slash or boatneck and no sleeves and was often made in a heavy, ornate brocade. There may have been a dramatic oversized bow or other detail to accentuate the shape. Alternatively, a dress might have a fitted and boned bodice, either with no sleeves or three-quarter-length sleeves, and a wide skirt. The skirt was often supported by wired, starched, or net underskirts to hold it out, away from the body. To keep warm, women added a fur stole or short jacket. As in the day, they wore gloves and a hat and carried a purse.

In the 1960s, cocktail dresses followed the change to A-line and then the simple rectangular shifts or tunics seen in day wear. What they lacked in shape, they made up for in fabric and color. Brocades were popular, but sometimes transparent organza or chiffon layers covered an opaque shift. These are easy styles to make up in bright, artificial fabrics. Lining materials are suitable, with their glossy finish and vibrant colors.

WEDDINGS

Wealthier brides of the 1950s wore voluminous and extravagant dresses with a fitted bodice and wide skirt, supported by net or wired petticoats. The dress might have a high collar and buttons down the front, copying the shirtfront style popular with day dresses, or it might have a scooped neckline or wide shawl-like collar that left the shoulders bare. Many brides wore long veils.

Of course, not all women could afford an ornate bridal gown. Some chose a dress or suit that could be worn again, often in a pale color such as dove gray or light blue.

During the 1960s, fashion moved toward modernity, and more brides wore shorter, plainer dresses or suits consisting of a dress and coat. Those who did choose a long gown often opted for a wide neckline and a relatively narrow skirt. There was less adornment with lace, ribbons, and frills and more emphasis on the fabric, which might have a woven pattern or texture. Veils were shorter and sometimes attached to a small hat. Sleeves tended to be three-quarter length. In the late 1960s, some weddings became less formal still, and some celebrity weddings even made a point of their informality.

Right: Wearing a simple, plain dress with a matching, collarless jacket, Mia Farrow weds Frank Sinatra in 1966.

Right: In the 1950s, women wore formal evening dresses with strapless, boned bodices and full skirts. Red lipstick and the lavish use of eyebrow pencil completed the look.

BALL DRESSES AND PROM DRESSES

The 1950s produced some of the most elegant and sumptuous ball gowns and prom dresses. Strapless gowns with a boned, fitted bodice topped clouds of taffeta, organza, and tulle in fantasy dresses inspired by Hollywood movies. Today, they could be put together using a basque and lengths of net or tulle.

Long sheath dresses often had an outsize bow or draped fabric that fell from the shoulder or went across the body. These might be in clingy fabrics or narrow pleats that emphasized the shape of the body or tailored in less flimsy fabrics but cut carefully to give a sculptural shape. An alternative to these curve-hugging styles was the "pumpkin" dress, a balloon of taffeta that gave no hint of a woman's shape at all.

During the 1960s, evening dresses and prom dresses began to lose their full skirts and eventually became quite straight and shift-like. Sheath dresses remained popular, often with a slit up the back. Floor-length tunics or shifts often had darts to give them shape but did not always mark the waist as had been universal in the 1950s. Square or scoop necks and sleeveless styles were common, but strapless dresses became a thing of the past.

Hair formally styled
in a chignon

Eye liner and
defined eyebrows

Bare shoulders

Long evening
gloves covering
the elbow

Small, handheld
evening purse

Wide skirt

1950s women's evening wear

Clip-on earrings

Short necklace

Boned, strapless bodice

Bright pink
brocade fabric

Layered and
stiffened net
petticoats

Matching satin sandals

CHAPTER 5

Men's Formal and Evening Dress

Men's formal wear during the daytime was principally a suit, which in the early 1950s was usually made of gray flannel and worn with a tie. In the evening, a formal occasion demanded a dinner jacket—tuxedo—with shirt, collar, and bow tie. During the 1960s, younger men moved away from formality for many occasions. But there were some new looks for formal events, and not everyone stuck to the main trends.

TAILCOATS AND TUXEDOS

A tailcoat, worn with a white shirt with a stiff collar and bow tie, was the most formal of outfits for men. It was worn to formal dances, dinners and weddings (as it still is now in some circles), and politicians were wearing

Below: As James Bond, actor Sean Connery looked his suave best in a white tuxedo and black bow tie.

LIBERACE GETS GLITTER

Pianist-entertainer Liberace's first deviation from regular formal wear came at a concert at the Hollywood Bowl in 1952, when he wore a white tailcoat. In Las Vegas, he replaced the tailcoat with a gold lamé jacket. Liberace's look was popular with audiences, and he soon added glittering jewelry and floor-length, colored fur coats. They became a trademark of his performances, which continued into the 1980s.

it to state occasions well into the 1960s. The tailcoat was also worn in dance/ musical movies (the black tailcoat had long been a trademark of dance star Fred Astaire, for example). In musicals, more often than in real life, it was paired with a top hat.

The tailcoat was cut high at the front but swooped down into two extended, pointed "tails" reaching the knees at the back. The jacket had wide satin lapels and decorative, rather than functional, buttons. It was worn open over a starched shirt and vest with a white bow tie. The shirt had a detachable "butterfly collar," which stood up against the neck and turned over only at the points beneath the chin.

The tuxedo, or dinner jacket, was less formal than the tailcoat. It was a hip-length, dark-colored jacket with flap pockets and a breast pocket, often with satin or silk lapels. It was worn buttoned over a starched white shirt with collar and with a black bow tie.

MESS DRESS

Most men spent some years in the armed forces during the 1950s and 1960s. For these men, formal dress meant mess uniform—a special dress uniform worn for formal occasions. The mess uniform varied between different branches of the service, countries, and ranks, but in general it was a variation of a short jacket and fitted trousers with a strip of braid down the outside leg seam. The jacket was adorned with braid and insignia and often worn over a colored vest or cummerbund. A mess uniform may have included a lined cape or coat, and always had a formal cap with braid and insignia. It was worn with a white shirt and a bow tie. In summer, the mess uniform was often white. The winter uniform would incorporate the colors of the force and regiment. Any re-enactment that involves a mess uniform should be carefully researched, since small differences in style have significant meanings in terms of rank and regiment.

Above: Actor and dancer Fred Astaire is perfectly turned out in formal top hat, black tailcoat, stiffened white shirt with butterfly collar, and white gloves.

DUDES AND RUDE BOYS

An American look, the outfit of dudes was smart and dandyish. Their suits had a long, five-buttoned jacket and high-waisted pants with pleats and cuffs, similar to zoot suits. They wore white socks, white buckskin shoes, and hats. The singer, Little Richard, wore an exaggerated version of dude clothing.

With their roots in Jamaica, rude boys adopted a stylish form of dress consisting of sharp suits, thin ties, and porkpie or trilby hats. Rude boys modeled themselves and their outfits on American gangster movies.

Right: The singer Little Richard wears a 1950s version of the zoot suit. His use of flashy clothes, pomaded hair, and makeup was inspired by 1940s blues singer Billy Wright.

ZOOT SUITS

The zoot suit became popular in the 1930s and 1940s among African Americans. By the 1950s, black, Hispanic, and Filipino Americans and Mexican immigrants were wearing it. The zoot suit had a long, voluminous jacket with wide lapels and broad, padded shoulders and high-waisted pants with peg legs—wide at the top but tapering to the ankle. It was worn with a hat, sometimes adorned with a feather, and thick-soled, pointed shoes, often in two colors (two tone). A gold watch chain was strung from the belt to below the bottom of the coat and back up to the breast pocket. Because the suit was expensive, requiring lots of fabric and expert tailoring, it was generally kept for "best" and worn to dances and parties.

In the 1950s, a watered-down version of the early, very baggy zoot suit was adopted by fashion designers and marketed to white Americans. A significant element of the dude look, it fed into the teddy boy style in Britain.

OVER THE TOP

In the 1950s, rock and roll grew as a phenomenon and popular musicians became idols and celebrities. During the 1950s and 1960s, some music stars wore increasingly extravagant outfits that were never likely to be seen on the streets. Elvis Presley wore gold lamé or sequined costumes, and Liberace developed his trademark look of camp extravagance.

FOREIGN INFLUENCE

Until the early 1960s, many people dressed formally for evening events, but, from the mid-1960s on, clothing became more casual. In place of the tuxedo, the Nehru jacket became popular. Based on the coat worn by Indian prime minister Jawaharlal Nehru, it is a jacket with a small, stand-up collar (called a mandarin collar), worn buttoned down the front. The Beatles wore Nehru jackets in 1965, as did movie villains—in particular the deadly opponents of James Bond!

MAKE IT—A GOLD LAMÉ SUIT

For an extravagant entertainer costume, buy a white tuxedo from a thrift shop and spray it with gold paint. Sew or glue on sequins for extra sparkle. If you want to cover the jacket with sequins, the easiest way is to use spray glue and sprinkle the sequins. Spray small areas at a time and press the sequins down firmly before the glue dries. You can also decorate jackets with feathers, plaster pearls, and fake gems available from costume shops.

Left: The actor Richard Harris, shown here completely on-trend in 1968, in a velvet Nehru jacket, bandana, and aviator shades.

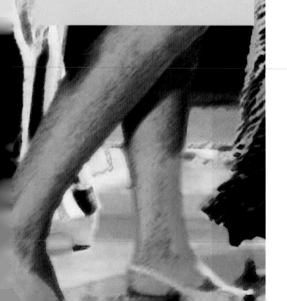

CHAPTER 6

Time Off—Leisure Wear

Suddenly, in the 1950s, people had leisure time—a welcome novelty after the hard war years. They spent it enjoying themselves: traveling, playing sports, dancing, and going to the beach. They wore clothes suited to these activities.

NIGHTCLUBS AND DISCOS

During the mid-1960s, outlandish, space-age-style clothes were sometimes worn to evening events, including dances and parties, but were too impractical to wear during the workday. The new discos and nightclubs gave young people somewhere to wear their more bizarre fashions. Clothes made of PVC, metal, plastic, and other experimental materials came into their own in the fashionable nightclubs of London, New York, and other large cities. White and silver were the predominant colors. Sequins, metal, and all things shiny were popular.

Above: Young women dance in miniskirts and dresses at a disco in the 1960s. Flat shoes or boots made dancing easy.

TRAVEL

Travel by train was popular in the 1950s and 1960s, but an increasing number of people owned cars or motorcycles. Men with motorcycles could look to any number of screen idols as models. A leather jacket, jeans, and a T-shirt were the bikers' uniform. Special clothes were designed to make driving more comfortable—especially in unheated cars. The three-quarter-length car coat was loose, with turned-back lapels and buttoned straps at the wrist and the back. A warmer alternative was a three-quarter-length sheepskin coat with leather buttons. On hotter days, a casual knitted jacket with a suede yoke and ribbed cuffs and waist was popular. Driving gloves were made of leather, with holes in the fingers and a larger hole over the back of the hand for ventilation.

SPORTS

The rise of television helped to spread interest and participation in sports. Tennis was very popular in the 1950s and 1960s. Women wore tennis dresses with short skirts, often pleated to allow freedom of movement. White ankle socks and white tennis shoes were essential. The skirt became progressively shorter throughout the 1950s and 1960s. For men, tennis wear was a white shirt and white shorts, which were generally quite baggy and cut long. In different colors, the same style of shorts was used for most other sports, from running and soccer to basketball.

ON THE SLOPES

In the 1950s, only the rich could afford to go skiing. Ski wear, without the light padding available now, was heavy and depended for warmth on thick fabrics. Knickers made of leather and thick, knitted socks were topped by a padded jacket that, for women, could be a roomy blouson of padded silk. Alternatively, thick wool trousers, waterproofed and gathered at the ankle, could be worn with a similar thick, waterproofed, zip-up jacket.

Above: 1960s fashion on the ski slopes included tight knickers or pants and thick jackets.

DANCING QUEENS

In the 1950s, the increasing popularity of vinyl records made DJs and discos possible, and more young people went out dancing in the evening. Circular skirts, pinched in and belted at the waist, were worn with a skintight round neck or turtleneck sweater or a crisp white blouse. This was a spectacular shape for dancing to the new rock-and-roll

MAKE IT— A CIRCULAR SKIRT

A circular skirt is easy to make from a circle of fabric with a doughnut-like hole cut in the center. The inside circumference should match the wearer's waist size. The skirt needs a single seam, with a zipper in the top part, and should be stitched onto a waistband. A white shirt with short sleeves and tapered in at the waist is easy to find or adapt; a polo shirt could be fitted to the body with darts. A net petticoat can be made from gathered bands or circles of net fashioned into a simple skirt with an elasticized waist.

Above: In the 1950s there was a brief craze for "poodle skirts." A garment such as this can easily be achieved by adding a poodle shape cut from felt to a circular skirt using appliqué or even fabric glue.

bands, twirling out over layers of stiff petticoats made from the new, inexpensive nylon net. Flat, round-toed shoes or low-heeled, strappy sandals made dancing easy. They were often worn with short white ankle socks, turned at the top.

IN THE SWIM

Women's swimwear in the 1950s was an offshoot of the corsetry industry. Swimsuits were structured and sturdy, with bra cups and zippers in the back. They were always one-piece—bikinis were reserved for movie stars and models since ordinary women considered them too risqué.

Swimsuits were either strapless or had thin straps. They had a stretch panel over the stomach that helped to hold the tummy in. They could be made of lined cotton, early stretch fabrics, or ruched nylon. Swimsuits were always cut straight across the top of the leg and usually had a modesty apron, which looked like a very short skirt, covering the top of the thighs. Women's swimming caps, made of rubber or plastic, were often decorated with plastic leaves and flowers, thought to look better than a bald-head-style hat. Men's swimwear in the 1950s was modest, consisting of quite long, baggy shorts, usually with a drawstring waist but sometimes elasticized.

STRE-E-E-TCH

Stretchy fabrics changed the look of swimwear in the 1960s. The zipper disappeared, and the swimsuit could simply be pulled on. Foreshadowing the bikini, the swimsuit became briefer. From the mid-1960s, a mesh panel in the sides or across the midriff or cutouts under the arms became common. Some swimsuits were essentially a two-piece held together with plastic rings between the top and bottom parts.

BEACHWEAR

Other beachwear for women in the 1950s consisted of a top and fitted shorts or, later in the decade, a "playsuit." The playsuit was one piece with a sleeveless or fitted strapless top and shorts or a short skirt with integral pants. It was made in brightly colored fabric, often spotted or striped. A nautical theme was popular, with red, white, and blue and sometimes sailor collars. Flat, strappy sandals made walking on sand easy.

For men, during the 1950s an exciting new pastime arrived, especially on the West Coast— surfing. Beachwear suddenly became much more important, with a surge of bright, flowery, and patterned tropical or Hawaiian shirts, worn most often with Bermuda shorts or sometimes light slacks. The shirt had short sleeves and was worn open at the neck, with a turned-back collar. It was paired with sunglasses, a new fashion item in the 1950s.

Right: This 1950s bikini has high-waisted pants and a "modesty skirt."

CHAPTER 7

Work Wear and Uniforms

In the 1950s, women returned to traditional roles after the turmoil of the war years. Many stayed at home; others worked as nurses, teachers, nannies, or housekeepers or in offices as typists and secretaries, and women also worked in the service industries as waitresses, cleaners, and chambermaids. Men, meanwhile, returned to their jobs in factories and offices and working the land. For much of the 1950s and 1960s, all young men had to serve for a few years in the armed forces, and during this time they wore military uniforms.

Above: Rock legend Elvis Presley joined the US Army in 1958. He served for nearly two years and was promoted to the rank of sergeant.

WOMEN'S UNIFORMS

Women's uniforms most often needed in re-enactments are those of nurses, waitresses, or domestic staff. Nurses' uniforms varied according to the particular hospital but generally consisted of a fitted dress with a flared or A-line skirt, short sleeves, and a flat, white collar. This was

46

worn with a large white apron and a starched white cap, flat shoes, and elasticized white armbands. The design of the cap and apron varied, too. In the early 1950s, the bib of the apron often extended over the shoulders with wide straps in an inverted triangle from the waist, covering the whole chest. In the 1960s, the bib was generally rectangular. Outerwear was a dark-colored wool cape, often with a contrasting lining.

A simple checked or striped dress of the type often worn by waitresses in diners can form the basis of a nurse's uniform for a re-enactment. The apron is easily fashioned from white cotton and requires only basic sewing skills. The bottom of the apron may be cut as a rectangle and gathered into a wide waistband. It must extend around the sides so that all of the skirt is covered. The bib is then stitched onto the waistband. The waistband ends in wide tapes to tie the apron at the back. Starching the apron will make it stiffer. A cap can be made from thick paper or card. Shoes must be flat and black or white.

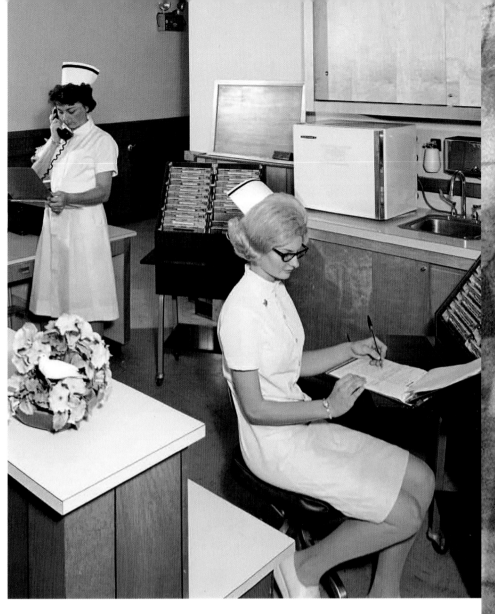

Above: In the 1960s, nurses in their white uniforms and starched caps communicated an impression of competence, authority, and professionalism.

Women in domestic service or working as waitresses also often wore starched aprons over a plain black or dark blue dress, maybe with a white collar. Some domestic servants wore their own clothes with an apron over the top. Since they were not well paid, their own clothes were a simple cotton dress or skirt and shirt following the general style of the day. Skirts were neither very full nor too tight—they needed to allow free movement but not use so much fabric as to be expensive.

WORKING MEN

Many men worked at hard manual labor and wore clothes that were functional and sturdy. These would often consist of jeans or thick cotton pants, heavy boots, and a T-shirt or tank top. In cold weather, men would

Right: In the role of a nurseryman in the 1955 movie *All That Heaven Allows*, Rock Hudson wears a red-checked work shirt to stunning Technicolor effect.

wear a thick cotton shirt and work jacket. The shirt frequently had a checked pattern. Things remained much the same in the 1960s, but from then on the boots were often Doc Martens.

Male office workers always wore a suit. The style of the suit changed during the 1950s and 1960s. In the 1950s, it was usually of gray flannel, loose-fitting, with a single-breasted jacket and wide trousers. It was worn with a white shirt and a detachable, white, starched collar and narrow tie. The cuffs were often starched. The trousers usually had cuffs, at least early in the decade, and were held up by suspenders. A vest matched the jacket and trousers. A fedora hat and plain, black shoes completed the outfit.

Other men, who did not need to wear a formal suit to work, wore trousers with cuffs, again held up by suspenders, and often a plain or checked shirt in a color that would not show dirt. These shirts had an integral collar and were not starched.

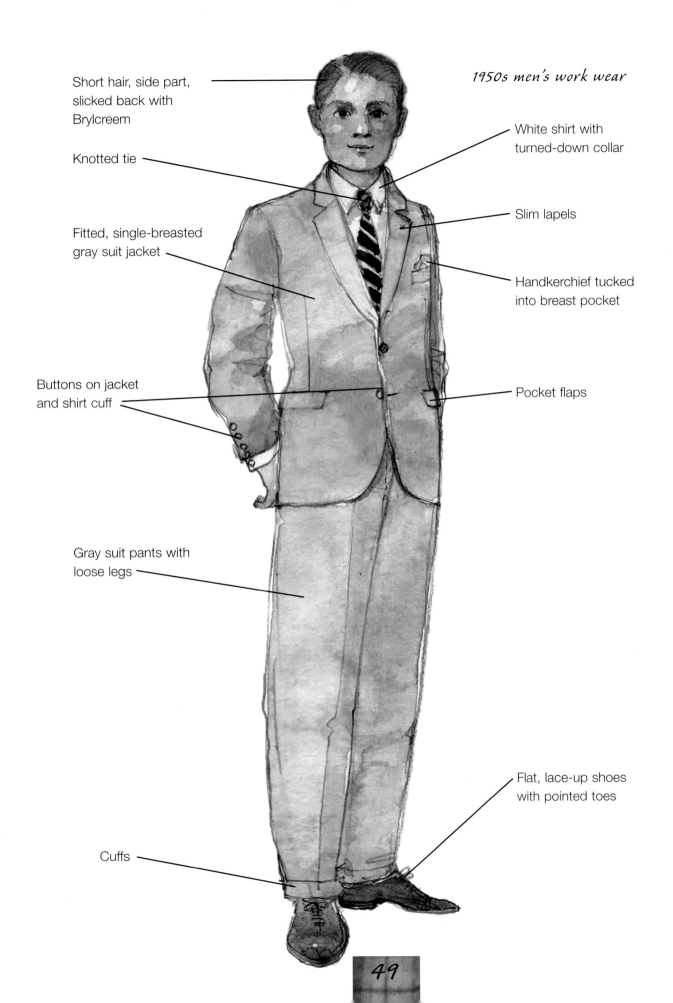

Short hair, side part, slicked back with Brylcreem

Knotted tie

Fitted, single-breasted gray suit jacket

Buttons on jacket and shirt cuff

Gray suit pants with loose legs

Cuffs

1950s men's work wear

White shirt with turned-down collar

Slim lapels

Handkerchief tucked into breast pocket

Pocket flaps

Flat, lace-up shoes with pointed toes

CHAPTER 8

Completing the Look

HIGH HEELS

" I don't know who invented the high heel, but all men owe him a lot. *"*

Marilyn Monroe

Attention to detail makes a look. In the 1950s and 1960s, many of the clothes worn by ordinary people going about their daily lives were not so very different from many of the clothes worn today. This makes it especially important to get the accessories, hair, and makeup right since they will make a costume convincing.

Above: A turban, pearls, gloves, sunglasses and purse are used here to accessorize an elegant two-piece; typically of the era, make-up is bold and immaculate.

UNDERNEATH

In the 1950s, women held in their figures with corsets and girdles. The "roll on" was a stretch girdle that extended from the waist to partway down the thighs. To keep control of areas higher up, a firm long-line bra held the bust in place and flattened any excess bulges between the bust and waist. Bras tended to have a conical, pointed shape.

During the 1960s, new fabrics and the less structured shape of clothes saw a move toward more flexible and comfortable underwear. Women still wore girdles, but the required body shape was flatter and more boyish. Men wore a simple tank top undershirt and baggy shorts or Y-front underpants.

HOSIERY

In the 1950s, pantyhose had not been invented—women wore stockings with garters. Stockings always had seams up the backs, and modern seamed pantyhose or stockings are still easy to find. With miniskirts, it was impossible to wear stockings and the newly designed pantyhose were essential. By the middle of the decade, pantyhose were available in thick and thin fabrics, with printed or woven patterns. Many similar styles are widely available today. Over-the-knee socks were also popular with miniskirts.

Men wore plain-colored socks, often held up with garters, during the 1950s. In the 1960s, new stretch fabrics allowed many men to abandon garters.

GLOVES

In the 1950s, a woman was not properly dressed without gloves. Wealthier women owned many pairs of gloves, often in different colors to coordinate with different outfits. White or cream gloves were highly regarded. This was because keeping them clean required an investment in time (often the maid's time) and therefore indicated that the gloves' owner had money. Although leather gloves were popular, many women wore cotton or nylon gloves since they were cheaper. For evening wear, gloves were long and could even reach beyond the elbow. Today, white evening gloves can be dyed to match an outfit.

Below: Marilyn Monroe in 1950s accessories— extravagant jewelry over full-length evening gloves.

Right: This fashion model from the 1960s wears long, zipped silver boots with Cuban heels.

SHOES

Shoes are a very important part of a look, particularly for women. Women's shoes changed a lot between 1950 and 1969. During the 1950s, women's shoes had a narrow heel and pointed toe. Slingbacks were popular. Heels were tapered and moderately high. Flat or low-heeled shoes, worn with slacks or for dancing, could be solid shoes or pointed slingbacks with a tiny heel.

The 1960s brought more variety to women's shoes. Heels became lower or disappeared altogether. Toes were still pointed at the start of the decade, but later a square or rounded toe became popular. The big innovation was boots for women. There was a craze for white leather knee-length or mid-calf boots. Eventually, boots made from shiny plastic even reached the thigh, ending just below the miniskirt. Fake snakeskin in black and white was used for shoes and boots for a while. Boots could also be in colored suede or leather.

Men's shoes in the 1950s were often simple lace-ups, but loafers were popular for informal wear. In the 1960s, the Chelsea boot became popular. This was a short, plain ankle boot with a low Cuban heel and a pointed "winkle-picker" toe, popularized by the Beatles. Later, men's boots—

like women's—had a squarer, chunky heel and square toe. Alternative footwear toward the end of the 1960s included flat leather sandals or flip-flops, Doc Martens work boots, or just bare feet.

HATS AND HEADGEAR

Women wore hats throughout the 1950s, often even indoors. Styles ranged from wide-brimmed "cartwheel" hats to flowerpot hats and cloches. Some had veils and called for even more pronounced makeup than usual so that the eyes and lips would remain prominent.
In the early 1960s, pillbox hats were popular. Later, berets, knitted or crocheted skullcaps, bubble-shaped toques, and caps were worn with tunics, shorts, and pants. When the "romantic" style took over, large floppy straw, raffia, or crocheted hats became fashionable.

Head scarves were popular in the 1950s and remained popular at least with older women in the 1960s. The scarf was folded into a triangle and knotted under the chin. Alternatively, a thin rectangular scarf could be wrapped around the head and neck. Hippies sometimes wore a long scarf tied around the head like a headband or a triangular scarf tied over the hair with the knot at the back of the neck.

Men wore hats most of the time during the 1950s, often a fedora, although caps were popular leisure wear. Younger men began to go bareheaded in the 1960s. Baseball caps began to be worn as fashion items in the United States.

ACCESSORIES

If a woman was to look properly dressed in the 1950s, her bag, shoes, belt, hat, and gloves needed to coordinate or match. As a result, a stylish woman had to have a large supply of accessories to go with all her outfits.

Right: First Lady, Jackie Kennedy, was a 1960s style icon. Here she wears a formal suit with matching pillbox hat, and gloves.

Below: Cardin's high-fashion extremes for men included wet-look thigh-high boots and belted tunics.

GLASSES AND SUNGLASSES

Sunglasses became popular during the 1950s. At the same time, prescription glasses began to be designed rather than purely functional. The characteristic shape for women's glasses in the 1950s had a heavy top frame, swept up at the outside corners.

During the 1960s, sunglasses with large frames in white or bright plastic and very dark lenses were in vogue. Later in the decade, hippie glasses had small, circular lenses with wire frames, a style popularized by John Lennon of the Beatles.

BAGS

In the 1950s, women always carried a purse. During the day, this would generally hang over the forearm and had a single strap. In the evening, a smaller clutch purse was more common. Most purses were of leather or sometimes crocodile skin. A distinctive alternative was a box-like purse made of Lucite, a hard acrylic that could have a shiny, translucent, or opalescent look. New styles of purses in the 1960s included leather satchels and purses and shoulder bags made of bright PVC or shiny

patent leather in different colors. White was popular. Hippies and romantics favored fabric shoulder bags or knitted, crocheted, or macramé bags made of yarn.

BELTS

In the 1950s, with the accent on women's waists, belts were naturally important accessories. Wide leather belts or belts in the same fabric as a woman's dress or coat were the most popular. Belts were of a straightforward design, with a metal buckle. During the 1960s, more adventurous belts appeared. With the dropped waist, belts were sometimes worn much lower. A wide, shiny, patent leather or PVC belt, often in white, was commonly worn with hipster pants by both women and men. Chain belts, which hung on the hips rather than cinched the waist, were worn over knitted dresses and tunics or shifts. They could be made of metal links or oversized plastic rings. Later in the decade, the romantic and hippie looks made use of scarves around the waist or hips and woven, crocheted, or macramé belts, often decorated with beads and feathers.

MAKEUP

In the 1950s and 1960s, fashionable women had very distinctive styles of makeup. In the 1950s, the eyes and lips featured prominently. Eyes were lined with black and flicked up at the corner. Brows were prominent, drawn over with eyebrow pencil. Eyelashes were accentuated, either with masses of mascara or with nylon false eyelashes. The skin was an even, pale tone. There was not yet any makeup formulated especially for black skin.

Women wore makeup whenever they went out of the house, though for many women the styles were not as exaggerated as those just described. They would wear rouge on their cheeks and lipstick on their mouths. Eye shadow in shades of blue and green was popular. Many

Below: Very pronounced eye makeup remained popular throughout the 1960s; hippies often added glitter or jewels.

Above: "The look" in 1960s makeup: pale skin, pale lips, and prominent eyes and brows.

"THE LOOK"

The addition of titanium to makeup in the 1960s made it possible to produce shimmering pale colors that soon came to be a defining feature of "the look" of the 1960s. Very pale lipsticks were worn, with heavy, dark eye makeup and white or very pale nail polish. The dark eyes with pale skin and lips produced a waif-like appearance popularized by icons such as Twiggy and Edie Sedgwick. Ostentatiously false eyelashes helped accentuate the eyes even more.

women continued to wear this style through the 1960s. Nails were painted either red or pink.

During the 1960s, the colors of makeup changed considerably. Skin was still pale, but so now were lips and nails. Eyes were made up to be wide, with thick, dark lashes, and were often still dark-rimmed, but paler eye shadows were also beginning to be used.

WOMEN'S HAIRSTYLES

In the 1950s, women kept their hair neat and often hidden under a hat when out and about. Long hair was pinned up in a chignon. Young, fashionable women might cut their hair short in the "pixie cut" popularized by Audrey Hepburn. From the mid-1950s, a trend for high ponytails emerged among teenagers. Older women kept the short, permed styles they had worn during the 1940s, held firmly in place with hair spray.

Band worn around head

Face painted with red dot on forehead, based on Hindu tradition

Long hair

Facial hair

Collarless loose shirt made of cheesecloth or light cotton

Necklace

Sleeveless Afghan vest

Leather shoulder bag with fringe

Braided hemp bracelet

Shabby, patched, widely flared bell-bottoms

Flip-flops

Face paint

Center-parted, long hair worn loose and unstyled

Ethnic jewelry

Button with political emblem

Pendant with yin-yang symbol

Long, fringed, and beaded vest

Indian cotton shirt

Braided leather belt

Long patchwork skirt

Beaded anklet

Bare feet

BACK-COMBING AND BEEHIVES

Beehive hairdos appeared late in the 1950s. A girl started by back-combing sections of hair (brushing it down toward the head) so that it stuck up in tufts. Then she gently brushed a top layer of hair smooth over the top. She used her hands to roll the hair into a chignon and pinned it in place. Hair spray made the style rock solid and slightly glossy. The "do" was wrapped in a scarf before bed. A girl maintained her beehive for as long as she could since it was too difficult to refashion it every day.

In the 1960s, young women began to wear their hair loose. It was often cut to shoulder length, maybe held back with a head band, and frequently given volume by back-combing. A more spectacular style, which required hair to be at least shoulder length, was the beehive—a massive, cotton-candy-like construction of back-combed hair.

The geometric patterns popular in fabric design from the mid-1960s were echoed in geometric haircuts, which often took the form of sleek, asymmetric bobs. African-American women sometimes straightened their hair to achieve the look. Later in the decade, long, loose hair became popular, often given a pre-Raphaelite look by braiding while wet to go with the nostalgic long skirts and frilled blouses. Hippies also wore their hair long and sometimes adorned it with tiny plaits or braids decorated with colored yarn and beads.

Below: Set in 1962, the movie *Hairspray* (2007) was a riot of back-combed hair and beehive hair styles.

MEN'S HAIRSTYLES

In the early 1950s, men wore their hair short and neat, cut above the ears. During the decade, hair became one of the identity badges of the different groups. One style popular with greasers and teddy boys was known as the DA ("duck's arse"). To achieve this style, the hair was parted at the back and each side was rolled in toward the center parting. At the front, the hair stood up in a pompadour. To keep it in shape, the hair was slicked with Brylcreem, giving it a greasy look.

The Beatles' "mop top" haircuts were at first seen as rebellious and untidily long, but hair soon became even longer. By the end of the decade, young men's hair often curled onto their shirt collars and beyond and was cut with as much care and attention as women's.

"Afro" hair was hair grown long and left to curl naturally so that it produced a mop of hair standing out from the head in all directions. It became a symbol of African-American pride.

Above: 1950s hairstyles in the movie *Grease* (1978).

FACIAL HAIR

Most men remained clean-shaven, but goatee beards and droopy mustaches became popular among the beat generation. Hippies allowed hair on their heads and faces to grow without restraint, and many hippies had a full beard as well as long hair.

Glossary

asymmetrical Not symmetrical; having a different shape or design on the left and right sides.

batik A technique for creating a pattern that involves covering parts of the fabric with wax before dyeing it. The parts covered with wax remain undyed; the wax is then removed by melting it.

Brylcreem A hair care product often used by men in the 1950s to give a greasy, wet look and hold a hairstyle in position.

capitalist A political and economic system characterized by free market economics, private ownership of businesses, and the drive to make a profit from invested capital.

capri pants Loose cropped pants for women, tapered to the mid calf.

clocks Designs on the sides of socks.

clothing coupons Paper coupons issued during and after World War II, which had to be presented, with money, in order to buy clothing. Each person had an allowance of coupons and could only buy clothes up to that limit.

Cold War A period of hostility and political tension between the United States and western allies and the USSR in the aftermath of World War II. Both sides stockpiled arms but there was no armed conflict.

conscription Forcible enrollment of young men into the armed forces for a period of service.

Cuban heel Short, square heels on men's boots.

drainpipes Very narrow, tight-fitting pants.

dude Smartly dressed city man.

FBI Federal Bureau of Investigation—part of the U.S. justice department which investigates crime.

fedora A soft felt hat with a creased crown and a snap-brim.

foulard tie A tie with a repeating pattern of a small geometric motif on a solid colored background.

lamé A fabric woven of flat metallic thread, usually gold or silver.

macramé Decorative knotting used to make belts, fringes, etc. from yarn or string.

moccasin A soft leather shoe, traditionally made from a single piece of leather gathered on top of the foot, but later a soft slipper-like shoe.

nuclear arms race The aggressive building and stockpiling of nuclear weapons by the United States and USSR during the 1950s and 1960s.

Peter Pan collar A flat, round collar which lies flat on a dress, blouse, or jacket.

pompadour A man's hairdo in which the hair is combed into a high mound in front.

ruching Decorative gathering.

scooter coat A short, straight coat often worn by teenagers riding scooters.

service industries Industries, such as restaurants and hotels, that provide services rather than goods.

snap-brim A flexible brim on a hat, which can be turned up and down.

swing coat A wide, triangular-shaped coat which hangs from a shoulder yoke.

toque A close-fitting hat or headdress with no brim. It is often made of soft, drapable fabric.

tulle A fine, fluid fabric made of silk, rayon or nylon.

twill A fabric woven with diagonal lines of threads crossing the warp (lengthwise) threads.

winkle picker Shoes or boots with very narrow, pointed toes, popular in the mid-twentieth century.

wool suiting A thick, woven wool fabric used to make tailored suits.

worsted A hardwearing, woven wool fabric, first made in the town of Worsted in Norfolk, England.

Further Information

BOOKS

Breward, Christopher, David Gilbert and Jenny Lister. *Swinging Sixties*. V&A Publications, 2006.

Brown, Mike. *The 1950s Look: Recreating the Fashions of the Fifties*. Sabrestorm, 2008.

Ettinger, Roseann. *Psychedelic Chic*. Schiffer, 1999.

Howell, Georgina. *In Vogue*. Penguin, 1975.

Miller, Judith. *Sixties Style*. Dorling Kindersley, 2006.

Olian, JoAnne. *Everyday Fashions of the Sixties: As Pictured in Sears Catalogs*. Dover, 2003.

Peacock, John. *The 1950s* (Fashion Sourcebooks). Thames & Hudson, 1998.

Peacock, John. *The 1960s* (Fashion Sourcebooks). Thames & Hudson, 1998.

Perry, George. *London in the Sixties*. Pavilion, 2001.

Ruby, Jennifer. *Costume in Context: The 1940s and 1950s*. Batsford, 1989.

Ruby, Jennifer. *Costume in Context: The 1960s and 1970s*. Batsford, 1989.

Schooling, Laura. *50s Fashion*. Taschen, 2007.

Schooling, Laura. *60s Fashion: Vintage Fashion and Beauty Ads*. Taschen, 2007.

Shih, Joy. *Funky Fabrics of the Sixties*. Schiffer, 1998.

YOUNGER READERS

Callan, Jim. *America in the 1960s* (Decades of American History series). Facts On File, 2005.

Carrick Hill, Laban. *America Dreaming: How Youth Changed America in the '60s*. Little, Brown, 2008.

Feinstein, Stephen. *The 1950s from the Korean War to Elvis*. Enslow, 2006.

Feinstein, Stephen. *The 1960s from the Vietnam War to Flower Power* (Decades of the 20th Century in Color). Enslow, 2006.

Lescott, James. *The Fifties in Pictures*. Parragon, 2007.

Lescott, James. *The Sixties in Pictures*, Parragon, 2007.

Powe-Temperley, Kitty. *The Sixties: Mods and Hippies*. Heinemann, 2000.

Tames, Richard. *The 1950s* (*Picture History of the 20th Century* series). Sea to Sea Publications, 2005.

Thomson, Neil. *The Sixties* (*When I Was Young* series). Franklin Watts, 2005.

Wills, Charles A. *America in the 1950s* (*Decades of American History* series). Facts On File, 2006.

WEB SITES

www.centuryinshoes.com/decades/ 1950/1950.html
Shoes styles from the 1950s and 1960s.

www.fashion-era.com/1950s/index.htm
Comprehensive resource on all aspects of fashion in the 1950s.

www.fashion-era.com/1960-1980.htm
Comprehensive resource on all aspects of fashion in the 1960s.

www.fashion-templates.com/about/1960
All about fashion and popular culture in the 1960s and 1950s.

www.frockery.co.uk
Buy 1960s clothes online (UK).

www.paperpast.com/html/fashion. html/www.fiftiesweb.com
Year-by-year guide to changes in fashion.

www.vam.ac.uk/vastatic/microsites/1211_ sixtieshistory_page.htm
A quick run-down on fashion and culture in the 1960s from the Victoria and Albert Museum, London.

www.vintageblues.com/history_main.htm
History of fashion in the 1900s. The site also has information and links related to buying vintage clothing.

Source List

A selection of plays, movies, TV series, and musicals that show clothing styles of the 1950s and 1960s.

PLAYS

Billy Liar (1960) by Keith Waterhouse and Willis Hall

Black Comedy (1965) by Peter Shaffer

The Caretaker (1959) by Harold Pinter

The Knack (1962) by Ann Jellicoe

Look Back in Anger (1956) by John Osborne

MOVIES AND TV

MADE IN THE 1950S

All That Heaven Allows (1955), dir. Douglas Sirk, with Rock Hudson, Jane Wyman

Breakfast at Tiffany's (1961) dir. Blake Edwards, with Audrey Hepburn, George Peppard

La Dolce Vita (1960), dir. Federico Fellini, with Marcello Mastroianni, Anita Ekberg

Dragnet (1956–9) dir. Jack Webb, with Jack Webb, Ben Alexander (TV series)

East of Eden (1955), dir. Elia Kazan, with Raymond Massey, James Dean

I Love Lucy (1951–7), dir. various, with Lucille Ball, Desi Arnaz (TV series)

The Man in the Gray Flannel Suit (1956), dir. Nunnally Johnson, with Gregory Peck, Fredric March

North by Northwest (1959), dir. Alfred Hitchcock, with Cary Grant, Eva Marie Saint

On the Beach (1959), dir. Stanley Kramer, with Gregory Peck, Ava Gardner

On the Waterfront (1954), dir. Elia Kazan, with Marlon Brando, Eva Marie Saint

Perry Mason (1957–66), dir. various, with Raymond Burr, William Hopper (TV series)

Rear Window (1954), dir. Alfred Hitchcock, with James Stewart, Grace Kelly

Rebel Without a Cause (1955), dir. Nicholas Ray, with James Dean, Natalie Wood

Saturday Night and Sunday Morning (1960), dir. Karel Reisz, with Albert Finney, Shirley Anne Field

A Streetcar Named Desire (1951), dir. Elia Kazan, with Marlon Brando, Vivien Leigh

Vertigo (1958), dir. Alfred Hitchcock, with James Stewart, Kim Novak

DEPICTING THE 1950S

Back to the Future (1985), dir. Robert Zemeckis, with Michael J. Fox, Christopher Lloyd

Far From Heaven (2002), dir. Todd Haynes, with Julianne Moore, Dennis Quaid

Forrest Gump (1994), dir. Robert Zemeckis, with Tom Hanks, Robin Wright

The Godfather, Parts 1 and II (1972, 1974), dir. Francis Ford Coppola, with Al Pacino, Marlon Brando

Indiana Jones and the Kingdom of the Crystal Skull (2008), dir. Steven Spielberg, with Harrison Ford, Cate Blanchett

The Last Picture Show (1971) dir. Peter Bogdanovich, with Timothy Bottoms, Jeff Bridges

Stand by Me (1987), dir. Rob Reiner, with Wil Wheaton, River Phoenix

The Talented Mr. Ripley (1999), dir. Anthony Minghella, with Matt Damon, Jude Law

MADE IN THE 1960S

Alfie (1966), dir. Lewis Gilbert, with Michael Caine, Vivien Merchant

Bewitched (1964–72), dir. various, with Elizabeth Montgomery, Agnes Moorhead (TV series)

Blow-Up (1966), dir. Michelangelo Antonioni, with David Hemmings, Sarah Miles

Doctor No (1962), dir. Terence Young, with Sean Connery, Ursula Andress

Dr. Kildare (1961–6), dir. various, with Richard Chamberlain, Leslie Nielsen (TV series)

Easy Rider (1969), dir. Dennis Hopper, with Dennis Hopper, Peter Fonda

Get Smart (1965–70), dir. various, with Don Adams, Barbara Feldon (TV series)

Goldfinger (1964), dir. Guy Hamilton, with Sean Connery, Honor Blackman

The Graduate (1967), dir. Mike Nichols, with Dustin Hoffmann, Anne Bancroft

Green Acres (1965–71), dir. Richard L. Bare, Ralph Levy, with Eddie Albert, Eva Gabor (TV series)

I Love You, Alice B. Toklas! (1968), dir. Hy Averback, with Peter Sellers, Jo Van Fleet

The Italian Job (1969), dir. Peter Collinson, with Michael Caine, Noel Coward

Ladybug, Ladybug (1963), dir. Frank Perry, with Jane Connell, William Daniels

The Man From U.N.C.L.E. (1964–8), dir. various, with Robert Vaughn, David McCallum (TV series)

Rowan and Martin's Laugh-In (1967–73), dir. Gordon Wiles, Mark Warren, with Dan Rowan, Dick Martin (TV series)

77 Sunset Strip (1958–64), dir. various, with Efrem Zimbalist Jr., Roger Smith (TV series)

A Taste of Honey (1961), dir. Tony Richardson, with Rita Tushingham, Dora Bryan

DEPICTING THE 1960S

American Graffiti (1973), dir. George Lucas, with Richard Dreyfus, Ron Howard

Animal House (1978), dir. John Landis, with John Belushi, Jim Matheson

Hairspray (2007), dir. Adam Shankman, with John Travolta, Michelle Pfeiffer

Hideous Kinky (1998), dir. Gillies MacKinnon, with Kate Winslet, Saïd Taghmaoui

I Wanna Hold Your Hand (1978), dir. Robert Zemeckis, with Nancy Allen, Bobby Di Cicco

JFK (1991), dir. Oliver Stone, with Kevin Costner, Tommy Lee Jones

The Krays (1990), dir. Peter Medak, with Gary Kemp, Martin Kemp

Mad Men (2007), dir. various, with Jon Hamm, Elisabeth Moss (TV series)

Malcolm X (1992), dir. Spike Lee, with Denzel Washington, Angela Bassett

Peggy Sue Got Married (1986), dir. Francis Ford Coppola, with Kathleen Turner, Nicolas Cage

Shampoo (1975), dir. Hal Ashby, with Warren Beatty, Julie Christie

Thirteen Days (2000), dir. Roger Donaldson, with Shawn Driscoll, Kevin Costner

The Wanderers (1979), dir. Philip Kaufman, with Ken Wahl, John Friedrich

Withnail and I (1987), dir. Bruce Robinson, with Richard E. Grant, Paul McGann

Woodstock (1970), dir. Michael Wadleigh (documentary)

MUSICALS

Grease (1978), dir. Randal Kleiser, with John Travolta, Olivia Newton-John

Hair (1979), dir. Milos Forman, with John Savage, Treat Williams

Quadrophenia (1979), dir. Frank Roddam, with Phil Daniels, Leslie Ash

West Side Story (1961), dir Jerome Robbins, Robert Wise, with Natalie Wood, Richard Beymer

Index

Numbers in **bold** refer to illustrations.